Transi

Words & Phrases

Abdullahi Hagar

Other books by Abdullahi Hagar

Emotions Thesaurus
Sentence Thesaurus
Dialogue Tags
Sentence Starters
Adjective Thesaurus
Adverb Thesaurus
Verb Thesaurus

A

aback *adverb*
Taken aback, I...

about *prep*
About that, I...

above *prep*
Above all, I...

abruptly *adverb*
Abruptly, I...

absently *adverb*
Absently, I...

absurdly *adverb*
Absurdly, I...

across *prep*
Halfway across, I...

addition *noun*
In addition, I...

admittedly *adverb*
Admittedly, I...

after *adverb*
Immediately after, I...
Shortly after, I...

after *prep*
After all, I...
After that, I...

After this, I...

afternoon *noun*
By late afternoon, I...
In the afternoon, I...
That afternoon, I...

afterthought *noun*
Almost as an afterthought, I...
As an afterthought, I...

afterward *adverb*
Shortly afterward, I...
Soon afterward, I...

afterwards *adverb*
Afterwards, I...

again *adverb*
Never again, I...
Not again, I...
Once again, I...
Then again, I...
Yet again, I...

ago *adverb*
Long ago, I...

ahead *adverb*
Up ahead, I...

air *noun*
Even from the air, I...

alarmed *adjective*
Alarmed, I...

alone *adjective*
Alone again, I...
Alone now, I...

Once alone, I...

alternative *noun*
With little alternative, I...
With no alternative, I...

although *prep*
Although, I...

amazement *noun*
To my amazement, I...

amused *adjective*
Amused, I...

anger *noun*
Harnessing my anger, I...

angry *adjective*
Angry now, I...

annoyed *adjective*
Annoyed, I...

answer *noun*
In answer, I...
When there was no answer, I...
Without waiting for an answer, I...

answer *verb*
Without answering, I...

answering *noun*
Instead of answering, I...

anxiously *adverb*
Anxiously, I...

anything *noun*

If anything, I...

apparently *adverb*
Apparently, I...

apprehension *noun*
With a bit of apprehension, I...

apprehensive *adjective*
Apprehensive, I...

approach *verb*
As I approached, I...

appropriate *adjective*
Appropriate, I...

arm *noun*
Arms folded, I...
Crossing my arms, I...
Lifting my arm, I...

around *prep*
All around me, I...

arrive *verb*
When I arrived, I...

as *prep*
As always, I...
As before, I...
As ever, I...

astonishment *noun*
To my astonishment, I...

at *prep*
At once, I...
At that, I...

At this, I...

awake *adjective*
When I was awake, I...

awake *verb*
When I awoke, I...

away *adverb*
Right away, I...

awkwardly *adverb*
Awkwardly, I...

ax *noun*
Even with an ax, I...

B

back *noun*
Arching my back, I...
At my back, I...
Lying on my back, I...

back *verb*
Backing away, I...

background *noun*
In the background, I...

backyard *noun*
In the backyard, I...

bag *noun*
Reaching into my bag, I...

balance *noun*
Regaining my balance, I...

bathroom *noun*
In the bathroom, I...

beam *noun*
In the beam, I...

beam *verb*
Beaming, I...

bearings *noun*
Getting my bearings, I...

beat *noun*
After a beat, I...

After a long beat, I...

bed *noun*
In bed, I...
Lying in bed, I...

bedroom *noun*
In the bedroom, I...

before *prep*
Before long, I...
Before that, I...
Before this, I...
Before, I...

beginning *noun*
In the beginning, I...

behind *prep*
Behind me, I...

belatedly *adverb*
Belatedly, I...

bellow *verb*
Bellowing, I...

below *adverb*
Far below, I...

below *prep*
Below me, I...

bemused *adjective*
Bemused, I...

bend *verb*
Bending down, I...
Bending over, I...

beside *prep*
Beside me, I...
Beside this, I...

besides *prep*
Besides that, I...
Besides, I...

beyond *prep*
Beyond that, I...

bit *noun*
After a bit, I...
Bit by bit, I...

bizarre *adjective*
Bizarre, I...

blindfolded *adjective*
Blindfolded, I...

blindly *adverb*
Blindly, I...

blink *verb*
Blinking, I...

blow *noun*
When the blow landed, I...

board *noun*
On board, I...

bottom *noun*
At the bottom, I...

bow *noun*
Dropping my bow, I...

bow *verb*
Bowing, I...

boy *noun*
As a boy, I...

brace *verb*
Bracing myself, I...

breakfast *noun*
After breakfast, I...

breath *noun*
Cursing under my breath, I...
Holding my breath, I...
Panting for breath, I...
Recovering my breath, I...
Sucking in a breath, I...
Taking a breath, I...
With a deep breath, I...

breathe *verb*
As I breathed, I...
Breathing hard, I...

breathless *adjective*
Breathless, I...

bridge *noun*
As I crossed the bridge, I...
At the bridge, I...

briefly *adverb*
Briefly, I...

button *verb*
As I buttoned up, I...

by *prep*
By now, I...
By that, I...
By then, I...

C

cab *noun*
From the cab, I...

call *noun*
Ending the call, I...
Killing the call, I...

calm *adjective*
Calm, I...

calm *noun*
In the calm, I...

calmly *adverb*
Calmly, I...

car *noun*
Once at the car, I...
When I reached the car, I...

care *noun*
With care, I...
With deliberate care, I...
With great care, I...

carefully *adverb*
Carefully, I...
Very carefully, I...

catch *verb*
When I was caught, I...

cathedral *noun*
Inside the cathedral, I...

cautiously *adverb*
Cautiously, I...
Very cautiously, I...

chair *noun*
Leaning back in my chair, I...
Sitting back in my chair, I...

chaos *noun*
In the chaos, I...

child *noun*
As a child, I...
When I was a child, I...

chuckle *verb*
Chuckling, I...

climb *verb*
As I climbed out, I...
As I climbed, I...

close *adverb*
So close, I...
Up close, I...

clumsily *adverb*
Clumsily, I...

college *noun*
In college, I...

come *verb*
Coming back, I...
When I came back out, I...
When I came back, I...
When I came out, I...

command *noun*
With a mental command, I...

composure *noun*
Regaining my composure, I...

conclusion *noun*
In conclusion, I...

confident *adjective*
Confident, I...

confidently *adverb*
Confidently, I...

confused *adjective*
Confused, I...
Though confused, I...

confusion *noun*
In the confusion, I...

conscious *adjective*
Barely conscious, I...

corner *noun*
Around the corner, I...

courage *noun*
Gathering my courage, I...

course *noun*
Of course, I...

credit *noun*
To my credit, I...

crouch *verb*
Crouching down, I...

Crouching, I...

cry *noun*
With a cry, I...

cry *verb*
Crying out, I...

curiosity *noun*
Out of curiosity, I...

curious *adjective*
Curious now, I...
Curious, I...

curse *noun*
With a curse, I...

curse *verb*
Cursing myself, I...
Cursing, I...

D

dark *noun*
After dark, I...
Even in the dark, I...
In the dark, I...

darkness *noun*
Even in the darkness, I...
In the darkness, I...
In total darkness, I...

dawn *noun*
At dawn, I...
By dawn, I...

day *noun*
A few days later, I...
After a few days, I...
All day long, I...
Days later, I...
During the day, I...
In the days that followed, I...
In the old days, I...
Later that day, I...
Most days, I...
One day, I...
Some days, I...
The next day, I...
The other day, I...
These days, I...
Throughout the day, I...

dazed *adjective*
Dazed, I...

death *noun*
Even in death, I...

decade *noun*
Decades ago, I...

defense *noun*
In my defense, I...

deliberately *adverb*
Deliberately, I...

delighted *adjective*
Delighted, I...

desk *noun*
Across the desk from me, I...
Sitting at my desk, I...
When I reached my desk, I...

desperate *adjective*
Desperate, I...

desperately *adverb*
Desperately, I...

desperation *noun*
In desperation, I...
In frantic desperation, I...

despite *prep*
Despite myself, I...
Despite that, I...
Despite this, I...

determination *noun*
By sheer determination, I...

determinedly *adverb*
Determinedly, I...

die *verb*
Before I died, I...

difficulty *noun*
With some difficulty, I...

dimly *adverb*
Dimly, I...

dimness *noun*
In the dimness, I...

dinner *noun*
After dinner, I...
At dinner, I...
Over dinner, I...

disappointed *adjective*
Disappointed, I...

disbelief *noun*
In disbelief, I...

disconcerted *adjective*
Disconcerted, I...

discreetly *adverb*
Discreetly, I...

disgust *noun*
In disgust, I...

disgusted *adjective*
Disgusted, I...

dismay *noun*
To my dismay, I...

dismount *verb*
Dismounting, I...

disoriented *adjective*
Disoriented, I...

distance *noun*
Even at this distance, I...
Even from this distance, I...
From a distance, I...
In the distance, I...
In the far distance, I...
Off in the distance, I...

distantly *adverb*
Distantly, I...

distracted *adjective*
Distracted, I...

do *verb*
When I was done, I...

door *noun*
After I closed the door, I...
As I neared the door, I...
At the door, I...
Opening the door, I...
When I opened the door, I...
When the door opened, I...

doorway *noun*
At the doorway, I...

down *adverb*
Deep down, I...

downstairs *adverb*
Back downstairs, I...
Once downstairs, I...

downstairs *noun*
Before going downstairs, I...

draw *verb*
When I drew away, I...

dread *noun*
With dread, I...

dream *noun*
In my dream, I...
In my dreams, I...
In the dream, I...

dress *verb*
When I was dressed, I...

drive *verb*
As I drove, I...

drowsily *adverb*
Drowsily, I...

dumbfounded *adjective*
Dumbfounded, I...

dusk *noun*
In the gathering dusk, I...

dutifully *adverb*
Dutifully, I...

dye *verb*
Dying, I...

E

ear *noun*
In my ear, I...

easel *noun*
Getting up from the easel, I...

eat *verb*
As I ate, I...

effort *noun*
With an effort, I...
With effort, I...
With great effort, I...
With some effort, I...

elevator *noun*
In the elevator, I...

embarrassed *adjective*
Embarrassed, I...

embrace *verb*
As I accepted the embrace, I...

emerge *verb*
Emerging, I...

emotionally *adverb*
Emotionally, I...

end *noun*
At the end, I...
By the end, I...
In the end, I...

Near the end, I...

engine *noun*
Gunning my engine, I...

evening *noun*
Later that evening, I...
That evening, I...

example *noun*
For example, I...

except *prep*
Except, I...

exchange *noun*
In exchange, I...

excited *adjective*
Excited, I...

excitedly *adverb*
Excitedly, I...

excitement *noun*
Trembling with excitement, I...

exhale *verb*
Exhaling, I...

exhausted *adjective*
Exhausted, I...
Suddenly exhausted, I...

exhaustion *noun*
Despite my exhaustion, I...

expression *noun*
With a triumphant expression, I...

eye *noun*
Closing my eyes, I...
Eyes closed, I...
Opening my eyes, I...
Rolling my eyes, I...
Rubbing my eyes, I...
Shutting my eyes, I...
When I closed my eyes, I...
When I opened my eyes, I...

F

fact *noun*
In fact, I...

faintly *adverb*
Faintly, I...

fall *verb*
As I fell, I...

fast *adjective*
Lightning fast, I...

fear *noun*
Paralyzed by fear, I...
With growing fear, I...

fearful *adjective*
Looking fearful, I...

feeling *noun*
With a sinking feeling, I...

find *verb*
Finding nothing, I...

finger *noun*
With a finger, I...
With deft fingers, I...
With trembling fingers, I...

finish *verb*
When I finished, I...
When I was finished, I...

firelight *noun*
In the firelight, I...

first *adjective*
At first, I...

flame *noun*
In a spurt of flame, I...

flash *noun*
In a flash, I...

flashlight *noun*
Using my flashlight, I...

floor *noun*
On the floor, I...

flourish *noun*
With a flourish, I...

flush *adjective*
With a flush, I...

flush *verb*
Flushing, I...

foot *noun*
Flipping back to my feet, I...
Getting to my feet, I...

for *prep*
For another, I...
For now, I...
For once, I...
For that, I...
For this, I...

frantic *adjective*

Frantic, I...

frantically *adverb*

Frantically, I...

free *adjective*

When I was free, I...

from *prep*

From behind, I...
From here, I...
From somewhere, I...
From there, I...
From this, I...

frown *verb*

Frowning slightly, I...
Frowning, I...

frustrated *adjective*

Frustrated, I...

frustration *noun*

In frustration, I...

fume *verb*

Fuming, I...

funny *adjective*

Funny, I...

furious *adjective*

Furious, I...

G

gag *verb*
Gagging, I...

gas *noun*
Hitting the gas, I...

gasp *noun*
With a gasp, I...

gasp *verb*
Gasping, I...

gently *adverb*
Gently, I...
Very gently, I...

get *verb*
Getting closer, I...
Getting up, I...
When I got back, I...
When I got close, I...
When I got downstairs, I...
When I got here, I...
When I got home, I...
When I got out, I...

giggle *verb*
Giggling, I...

gingerly *adverb*
Gingerly, I...

give *verb*
Giving up, I...

glance *noun*
At first glance, I...
In a glance, I...
In a swift glance, I...
Without a backward glance, I...

glance *verb*
Glancing around, I...
Glancing back, I...
Glancing down, I...
Glancing up, I...
When I glanced up, I...

glass *noun*
Through the glass, I...

gloom *noun*
In the gloom, I...

go *verb*
As I went, I...
Wherever I went, I...

goodbye *noun*
After saying goodbye, I...

greedily *adverb*
Greedily, I...

grimace *verb*
Grimacing, I...

grimly *adverb*
Grimly, I...

grin *noun*
Suppressing a grin, I...

grin *verb*
Grinning, I...
Still grinning, I...

groan *noun*
With a groan, I...

groan *verb*
Groaning, I...

groggily *adverb*
Groggily, I...

groggy *adjective*
Groggy, I...

ground *noun*
Back on the ground, I...

growl *noun*
On a growl, I...
With a growl, I...

growl *verb*
Growling, I...

grumble *verb*
Grumbling, I...

grunt *noun*
With a grunt, I...

grunt *verb*
Grunting, I...

guiltily *adverb*
Guiltily, I...

gulp *verb*
Gulping, I...

gut *noun*
In my gut, I...

H

hallway *noun*
In the hallway, I...

haltingly *adverb*
Haltingly, I...

hand *noun*
Hand over hand, I...
In one hand, I...
On the other hand, I...
Using both hands, I...
With a shaking hand, I...
With a trembling hand, I...
With both hands, I...
With one hand, I...
With rough hands, I...
With shaking hands, I...
With trembling hands, I...

hang *verb*
After I hung up, I...
Hanging up, I...
When I hung up, I...

happen *verb*
When nothing happened, I...

haste *noun*
In my haste, I...

hastily *adverb*
Hastily, I...

hat *noun*
As for a hat, I...

haze *noun*
Moving into the haze, I...

head *noun*
Bending my head, I...
Head down, I...
In my head, I...
Inside my head, I...
Lifting my head, I...
Lowering my head, I...
On my head, I...
Raising my head, I...
Shaking my head, I...
Tilting my head, I...
Turning my head, I...
When I lifted my head, I...
When I shook my head, I...

hear *verb*
Hearing nothing, I...

heart *noun*
Heart hammering, I...
Heart pounding, I...
Heart racing, I...
Heart skipping, I...
Heart thumping, I...
In my heart, I...
With a sinking heart, I...

heat *noun*
Despite the heat, I...

heel *noun*
Spinning on my heel, I...

helpless *adjective*
Helpless, I...

helplessly *adverb*
Helplessly, I...

hesitantly *adverb*
Hesitantly, I...

hesitate *verb*
Without hesitating, I...

hesitation *noun*
After a brief hesitation, I...
After a long hesitation, I...
After some hesitation, I...
With no hesitation, I...
Without hesitation, I...

hill *noun*
Up the hill, I...

hindsight *noun*
In hindsight, I...

hip *noun*
Rolling my hips, I...
Swiveling my hips, I...

hold *noun*
Tightening my hold, I...

home *noun*
As I entered the home, I...
At home, I...
Before leaving home, I...
On the way home, I...
Once home, I...

hopefully *adverb*
Hopefully, I...

horror *noun*
In horror, I...
To my horror, I...
With horror, I...

hour *noun*
A few hours later, I...
After a couple of hours, I...
After an hour, I...
An hour later, I...
For hours, I...
For the next hour, I...
Hours ago, I...
Hours later, I...
Within an hour, I...

house *noun*
Back at the house, I...
In the house, I...

howl *verb*
Howling, I...

hurriedly *adverb*
Hurriedly, I...

I

idly *adverb*
Idly, I...

ignore *verb*
Ignoring him\her, I...

immediately *adverb*
Almost immediately, I...
Immediately, I...

imperceptibly *adverb*
Almost imperceptibly, I...

impulse *noun*
On an impulse, I...
On impulse, I...

impulsively *adverb*
Impulsively, I...

in *prep*
In that, I...
In this, I...

incensed *adjective*
Incensed, I...

incidentally *adverb*
Incidentally, I...

include *verb*
Including, I...

incredibly *adverb*
Incredibly, I...

inexplicably *adverb*
Inexplicably, I...

initially *adverb*
Initially, I...

inside *adverb*
Deep inside, I...
Once inside, I...

insight *noun*
In a flash of insight, I...

instance *noun*
For instance, I...

instant *noun*
An instant later, I...
For a brief instant, I...
For an instant, I...
In an instant, I...
In that instant, I...
In that same instant, I...
Just for an instant, I...

instantly *adverb*
Almost instantly, I...
Instantly, I...

instinct *noun*
On instinct alone, I...
On instinct, I...

instinctively *adverb*
Instinctively, I...

intellectually *adverb*
Intellectually, I...

investigation *noun*
After an investigation, I...

inwardly *adverb*
Inwardly, I...

irritated *adjective*
Irritated, I...

J

jab *verb*
As I jabbed, I...

jaw *noun*
Clenching my jaw, I...
Jaw dropping, I...

K

keep *verb*
Keeping low, I...

key *noun*
Without a key, I...

kid *noun*
When I was a kid, I...

kitchen *noun*
In the kitchen, I...
Leaving the kitchen, I...
When I entered the kitchen, I...
When I reached the kitchen, I...

knee *noun*
Looking down at my knees, I...

kneel *verb*
Kneeling down, I...
Kneeling, I...

L

landing *noun*
On the first landing, I...

last *adjective*
At last, I...

later *adverb*
Later on, I...

laugh *noun*
With a laugh, I...

laugh *verb*
Laughing, I...
Still laughing, I...

law *noun*
By law, I...

lean *verb*
Leaning back, I...
Leaning close, I...
Leaning down, I...
Leaning forward, I...
Leaning in, I...

leave *verb*
As I left, I...
Before I left, I...
Before leaving, I...
When I left, I...

left *noun*
To my left, I...

leg *noun*
Crossing my legs, I...

length *noun*
At length, I...

letter *noun*
In the letter, I...

level *noun*
On some level, I...

lie *verb*
Lying flat, I...

life *noun*
For the life of me, I...
In another life, I...
In life, I...
In my life, I...

light *noun*
In the dim light, I...

lightning *noun*
Quick as lightning, I...

lip *noun*
Biting my lip, I...
Pursing my lips, I...

listen *verb*
As I listened, I...

little *adjective*
When I was little, I...

look *verb*

As I looked around, I...
As I looked out, I...
Looking around, I...
Looking away, I...
Looking back, I...
Looking closer, I...
Looking down, I...
Looking out, I...
Looking over, I...
Looking round, I...
Looking up, I...
When I looked down, I...
When I looked up, I...
When I looked, I...
Without looking back, I...
Without looking, I...

lost *adjective*

Lost, I...

loudly *adverb*

Loudly, I...

luck *noun*

With a little luck, I...
With any luck, I...
With luck, I...

lunch *noun*

After lunch, I...
At lunch, I...

M

maneuver *verb*
After some maneuvering, I...

meantime *noun*
In the meantime, I...

meanwhile *noun*
In the meanwhile, I...

measure *noun*
For good measure, I...

mention *verb*
As I mentioned, I...

mercifully *adverb*
Mercifully, I...

methodically *adverb*
Methodically, I...

midnight *noun*
At midnight, I...

mile *noun*
After a mile, I...

mind *noun*
In my mind, I...

minute *noun*
A few minutes later, I...
A minute later, I...
After a couple of minutes, he...

After a few minutes, I...
After a minute or so, I...
After a minute or two, I...
After a minute, I...
After several minutes, I...
At the last minute, I...
For a long minute, I...
For a minute or two, I...
For a minute, I...
For the next several minutes, I...
In a matter of minutes, I...
In a minute, I...
In that minute, I...
Minutes later, I...
Several minutes later, I...
Within a few minutes, I...
Within minutes, I...

miracle *noun*
By some miracle, I...

miraculously *adverb*
Miraculously, I...

mirror *noun*
In the mirror, I...

mistake *noun*
Realizing my mistake, I...

moan *noun*
With a moan, I...

moment *noun*
A few moments later, I...
A moment later, I...
After a few moments, I...
After a long moment, I...
After a moment, I...
As of this moment, I...

At that moment, I...
At the last moment, I...
At the moment, I...
At the same moment, I...
At this moment, I...
For a brief moment, I...
For a long moment, I...
For a moment, I...
For an awful moment, I...
For long moments, I...
For the moment, I...
In a few moments, I...
In a moment, I...
In that moment, I...
In this moment, I...
Moments ago, I...
Moments later, I...
One moment, I...
Until that moment, I...
Until this moment, I...
Within moments, I...

month *noun*
A month ago, I...
For months, I...

moonlight *noun*
In the moonlight, I...

morning *noun*
By morning, I...
Each morning, I...
Every morning, I...
Good morning, I...
In the morning, I...
Next morning, I...
One morning, I...
The next morning, I...
This morning, I...
Tomorrow morning, I...

motion *noun*
In fluid motion, I...

mouth *noun*
Opening my mouth, I...

move *verb*
As I moved, I...
Moving closer, I...
Moving quickly, I...
Moving slowly, I...

N

naked *adjective*
Naked, I...
When I was naked, I...

near *verb*
As I neared, I...

necessary *adjective*
If necessary, I...

nervously *adverb*
Nervously, I...

night *noun*
After last night, I...
All night, I...
At night, I...
Every night, I...
Good night, I...
Last night, I...
Later that night, I...
One night, I...
That night, I...
The night before, I...
This night, I...
Tomorrow night, I...

nod *noun*
With a nod, I...

nod *verb*
Nodding, I...

noon *noun*
At noon, I...

normally *adverb*
Normally, I...

notice *verb*
Without even noticing, I...

now *adverb*
Even now, I...
From now on, I...
Right now, I...

numb *adjective*
Numb, I...

numbly *adverb*
Numbly, I...

O

obediently *adverb*
Obediently, I...

obviously *adverb*
Obviously, I...

odd *adjective*
Odd, I...

oddly *adverb*
Oddly enough, I...
Oddly, I...

of *prep*
Of late, I...
Of that, I...

office *noun*
In my office, I...

on *adverb*
Early on, I...

one-handed *adjective*
One-handed, I...

optimistic *adjective*
Optimistic, I...

order *noun*
In short order, I...

ordinarily *adverb*
Ordinarily, I...

outside *adverb*
Once outside, I...

outside *noun*
On the outside, I...

outside *prep*
Outside again, I...

outwardly *adverb*
Outwardly, I...

overwhelmed *adjective*
Overwhelmed, I...

P

pack *noun*
Shouldering my pack, I...

painfully *adverb*
Painfully, I...

pang *noun*
With a pang, I...

panic *noun*
After a moment of panic, I...
In a panic, I...
In panic, I...
Wild with panic, I...
With a thrum of panic, I...
With panic, I...

panic *verb*
Panicking, I...

panicked *adjective*
Panicked, I...

pant *verb*
Panting, I...

part *noun*
For my part, I...

particular *adjective*
In particular, I...

past *noun*
In the past, I...

pause *noun*
After a brief pause, I...
After a long pause, I...
After a pause, I...
After a slight pause, I...
After an uncomfortable pause, I...

pause *verb*
Pausing, I...
Without pausing, I...

perfect *adjective*
Perfect, I...

periphery *noun*
From my periphery, I...
In my periphery, I...

personally *adverb*
Personally, I...

phone *noun*
Over the phone, I...
When the phone rang, I...

photo *noun*
In the photo, I...

physically *adverb*
Physically, I...

piece *noun*
Piece by piece, I...

pleased *adjective*
Pleased, I...

point *noun*

At some point, I...
At that point, I...
At this point, I...
Until that point, I...

politely *adverb*
Politely, I...

preparation *noun*
As a final preparation, I...

present *adjective*
At present, I...

presentable *adjective*
When I was presentable, I...

pull *verb*
Pulling back, I...
When I pulled away, I...
When I pulled back, I...

pulse *noun*
Pulse pounding, I...
Pulse racing, I...

push *verb*
Pushing through, I...

puzzled *adjective*
Puzzled, I...

Q

question *noun*
Anticipating the question, I...

quickly *adverb*
Quickly, I...

quiet *adjective*
Quiet, I...

quietly *adverb*
Quietly, I...

R

reach *verb*
Reaching down, I...
Reaching forward, I...
Reaching inside, I...
Reaching out, I...
Reaching over, I...
Reaching overhead, I...
Reaching up, I...

ready *adjective*
When I was ready, I...

reality *noun*
In reality, I...

really *adverb*
Not really, I...

reason *noun*
For no good reason, I...

recover *verb*
When I recovered, I...

reflexively *adverb*
Reflexively, I...

release *verb*
Releasing him\her, I...

relieved *adjective*
Relieved, I...

reluctance *noun*
With reluctance, I...

reluctantly *adverb*
Reluctantly, I...

remarkably *adverb*
Remarkably, I...

reply *noun*
When there was no reply, I...
Without waiting for a reply, I...
Without waiting for his\her reply, I...

resist *verb*
Unable to resist, I...

resolute *adjective*
Resolute, I...

respect *noun*
With all due respect, I...
With respect, I...

response *noun*
In response, I...
When there was no response, I...
Without waiting for a response, I...
Without waiting for his\her response, I...

rest *noun*
As for the rest, I...

restless *adjective*
Restless, I...

retrospect *noun*
In retrospect, I...

return *noun*
In return, I...
On my return, I...

return *verb*
When I returned, I...

reverently *adverb*
Reverently, I...

ride *noun*
During the ride, I...

right *noun*
To my right, I...

rise *verb*
Rising, I...

roar *noun*
With a roar, I...

room *noun*
Across the room, I...
Before I left the room, I...
In the living room, I...

run *verb*
As I ran, I...

rush *noun*
In a rush, I...

S

sadly *adverb*
Sadly, I...

satisfied *adjective*
Apparently satisfied, I...
Satisfied, I...
When I was satisfied, I...

say *verb*
Before I could say anything,
he\she...
Needless to say, I...
Saying nothing, I...

school *noun*
At school, I...

scowl *noun*
With a scowl, I...

scowl *verb*
Scowling, I...

scramble *noun*
In a scramble, I...

scream *verb*
Screaming, I...

search *verb*
Searching, I...

seat *noun*
In the front seat, I...

In the passenger seat, I...
On the seat beside me, I...

second *adjective*
After a second, I...
For a second, I...
In the second, I...

second *noun*
A few seconds later, I...
A second later, I...
After a few seconds, I...
After several seconds, I...
At the last second, I...
For a few seconds, I...
For a second, I...
For a split second, I...
For one second, I...
For several seconds, I...
In seconds, I...
Seconds later, I...
With each passing second, I...
Within seconds, I...

see *verb*
Seeing him\her, I...

self-consciously *adverb*
Self-consciously, I...

selfishly *adverb*
Selfishly, I...

seriously *adverb*
Seriously, I...

shadow *noun*
In the shadows, I...

shake *verb*

Shaking, I...

shaken *adjective*
Shaken, I...

shame *noun*
To my shame, I...

shattered *adjective*
Shattered, I...

shiver *verb*
Shivering, I...

shock *noun*
To my shock, I...

short *adjective*
In short, I...

shoulder *noun*
Glancing over my shoulder, I...
Looking over my shoulder, I...
Over my shoulder, I...
Squaring my shoulders, I...

show *noun*
When the show ended, I...

shower *noun*
After a shower, I...
In the shower, I...

shriek *noun*
With a shriek, I...

shrug *noun*
With a shrug, I...

shrug *verb*
Shrugging, I...

shudder *noun*
With a shudder, I...

shudder *verb*
Shuddering, I...

shy *adjective*
Shy, I...

side *noun*
At my side, I...
On the far side, I...
On the other side, I...

sidewalk *noun*
From the sidewalk, I...

sigh *noun*
With a sigh, I...

sigh *verb*
Sighing, I...

silence *noun*
After a long silence, I...
In silence, I...
In the ensuing silence, I...
In the silence that followed, I...
In the silence, I...

silently *adverb*
Silently, I...

similarly *adverb*
Similarly, I...

since *prep*
Since then, I...

sip *noun*
Taking a sip, I...

sit *verb*
Sitting back down, I...
Sitting back, I...
Sitting up, I...
When I sat back down, I...
When I sat, I...

slave *noun*
As a slave, I...

sleep *verb*
Sleeping, I...
When I slept, I...

slowly *adverb*
Slowly, I...
Very slowly, I...

smile *noun*
With a smile, I...

smile *verb*
Smiling, I...
Still smiling, I...

snarl *noun*
On a snarl, I...
With a snarl, I...

snarl *verb*
Snarling, I...

sniffle *verb*

Sniffling, I...

snort *verb*
Snorting, I...

so *adverb*
Even so, I...

sob *noun*
With a sob, I...

sob *verb*
Sobbing, I...

softly *adverb*
Softly, I...

soon *adverb*
Pretty soon, I...
Soon enough, I...
Very soon, I...

speak *verb*
As I spoke, I...
When I spoke again, I...
When I spoke, I...
Without speaking, I...

specifically *adverb*
Specifically, I...

speechless *adjective*
Speechless, I...

speed *noun*
With lightning speed, I...

spellbound *adjective*
Spellbound, I...

spin *verb*
Spinning around, I...
Spinning low, I...
Spinning round, I...
Spinning, I...

squeal *verb*
Squealing, I...

squint *verb*
Squinting, I...

stairs *noun*
As I mounted the stairs, I...
Climbing the stairs, I...

stand *verb*
As I stood up, I...
Standing dead still, I...
Standing there, I...
Standing up, I...
Standing, I...

start *noun*
For a start, I...
With a start, I...

startled *adjective*
Startled, I...

statement *noun*
In my statement, I...
With that statement, I...

steel *verb*
Steeling myself, I...

step *noun*
After a few steps, I...

Step by step, I...
With each step, I...

step *verb*
Stepping back, I...
Stepping forward, I...
Stepping inside, I...
Stepping outside, I...
When I stepped inside, I...

still *adverb*
Even still, I...

stillness *noun*
In the stillness, I...

stool *noun*
Sitting down on the stool, I...

stop *noun*
At the last stop, I...

stop *verb*
Before I could stop myself, I...
When I stopped, I...

straighten *verb*
As I straightened, I...
Straightening, I...
When I straightened, I...

strangely *adverb*
Strangely, I...

stride *noun*
With a few strides, I...

struggle *noun*
During the struggle, I...

stunned *adjective*
Stunned, I...

stupid *adjective*
Stupid, I...

such *adjective*
As such, I...

suddenly *adverb*
Suddenly, I...

supper *noun*
After supper, I...

sure *adjective*
Soon after, I...
Sure enough, I...

surface *verb*
When I surfaced, I...

surprise *noun*
Blinking in surprise, I...
To my surprise, I...

surprised *adjective*
Surprised, I...

surprisingly *adverb*
Not surprisingly, I...
Surprisingly, I...

surrender *noun*
Faking surrender, I...

surreptitiously *adverb*
Surreptitiously, I...

swallow *verb*
Swallowing hard, I...

swear *verb*
Swearing, I...

sweat *noun*
Drenched in sweat, I...

sweat *verb*
Sweating, I...

swim *verb*
As I swam, I...

sword *noun*
Drawing my sword, I...
Sheathing my sword, I...

T

table *noun*
Beneath the table, I...

tenderly *adverb*
Tenderly, I...

tentative *adjective*
Tentative, I...

tentatively *adverb*
Tentatively, I...

terrified *adjective*
Terrified, I...

terror *noun*
Fighting my terror, I...
In terror, I...

thankfully *adverb*
Almost thankfully, I...

then *adverb*
Back then, I...
Even then, I...
From then on, I...
Just then, I...
Right then, I...

theory *noun*
In theory, I...

there *adverb*
Halfway there, I...
Once there, I...
Still there, I...

thing *noun*
All things considered, I...
For another thing, I...
The thing was, I...

think *verb*
Without thinking, I...

thinking *noun*
Almost without thinking, I...

though *adverb*
First though, I...
Now though, I...

thought *noun*
At that thought, I...
On second thought, I...
With that thought, I...
Without a second thought, I...
Without conscious thought, I...

threshold *noun*
At the threshold, I...

throat *noun*
Clearing my throat, I...

through *adverb*
Once through, I...

thumb *noun*
With my thumb, I...

time *noun*
After a long time, I...
After a short time, I...

After a time, I...
At another time, I...
At one time, I...
At the same time, I...
At the time, I...
At times, I...
By this time, I...
During that time, I...
Each time, I...
Except this time, I...
For a long time, I...
For a time, I...
For some time, I...
For the first time ever, I...
For the first time, I...
In a race against time, I...
In no time, I...
In time, I...
Last time, I...
Next time, I...
Once upon a time, I...
One time, I...
Over time, I...
Some time later, I...
Taking my time, I...
The first time, I...
The last time, I...
The second time, I...
The whole time, I...
This time, I...
Wasting no time, I...
When the time came, I...

tiptoe *noun*
Standing on tiptoe, I...

tiptoes *noun*
Pushing up onto my tiptoes, I...

today *noun*
After today, I...

token *noun*
By the same token, I...

tone *noun*
In terse tones, I...

tonight *adverb*
Earlier tonight, I...

tonight *noun*
After tonight, I...

tooth *noun*
Gritting my teeth, I...
Teeth gritted, I...
Through chattering teeth, I...

top *noun*
At the top, I...
When I reached the top, I...

tremble *verb*
Trembling, I...

troubled *adjective*
Troubled, I...

truth *noun*
In truth, I...

try *verb*
If I tried, I...

turn *verb*
Turning around, I...
Turning away, I...
Turning back, I...
Turning in, I...

42

Turning left, I...
Turning, I...
When I turned, I...
Without turning, I...

twist *verb*
Twisting around, I...

U

unbidden *adjective*
Unbidden, I...

uncertain *adjective*
Uncertain, I...

uncharacteristically *adverb*
Uncharacteristically, I...

unconscious *adjective*
Unconscious, I...

undaunted *adjective*
Undaunted, I...

uneasy *adjective*
Uneasy, I...

unexpectedly *adverb*
Unexpectedly, I...

unseen *adjective*
Unseen, I...

unsettled *adjective*
Unsettled, I...

unsteady *adjective*
Unsteady, I...

until *prep*
Until now, I...
Until then, I...

up *adverb*
Close up, I...
From up here, I...
Halfway up, I...

useless *adjective*
Useless, I...

usual *adjective*
As usual, I...

V

vigor *noun*
With renewed vigor, I...

vision *noun*
In the vision, I...

voice *noun*
In a halting voice, I...
In a somber voice, I...
Raising my voice, I...

wait *verb*
As I waited, I...
While I waited, I...

wake *verb*
When I woke again, I...
When I woke up, I...
When I woke, I...

walk *verb*
As I walked, I...

wall *noun*
Along the wall, I...
At the wall, I...

war *noun*
After the war, I...
Before the war, I...

warily *adverb*
Warily, I...

warning *noun*
With no warning, I...
Without warning, I...

watch *noun*
Looking at my watch, I...

watch *verb*
Watching him\her, I...

way *noun*

Along the way, I...
In an odd way, I...
On my way, I...
On the way, I...
Somewhere along the way, I...

weaponless *adjective*
Weaponless, I...

wearily *adverb*
Wearily, I...

week *noun*
A week later, I...
All week, I...
In the weeks that followed, I...
Last week, I...
Next week, I...
One week, I...
The week before, I...
Weeks later, I...

while *noun*
After a long while, I...
After a while, I...
For a long while, I...
For a while, I...

whim *noun*
On a whim, I...

whirl *verb*
Whirling, I...

whisper *noun*
In a whisper, I...

whistle *verb*
Whistling, I...

whole *noun*
On the whole, I...

wide-eyed *adjective*
Wide-eyed, I...

will *noun*
Against my will, I...

wince *verb*
Wincing, I...

window *noun*
From my window, I...
Through the window, I...

windshield *noun*
Through the windshield, I...

winter *noun*
In the winter, I...

wisely *adverb*
Wisely, I...

with *prep*
With that, I...
With, I...

within *prep*
Within, I...

wonder *noun*
In a state of wonder, I...

word *noun*
In a word, I...
Then without another word, I...
Without a word, I...

Without another word, I...

wordless *adjective*
Wordless, I...

wordlessly *adverb*
Wordlessly, I...

work *noun*
After work, I...

work *verb*
As I worked, I...
Working quickly, I...

wrist *noun*
Releasing my wrists, I...

Y

yawn *verb*
Yawning, I...

year *noun*
A year ago, I...
For years, I...
In the years that followed, I...
Last year, I...
One year, I...
Over the years, I...
Within a few years, I...
Years ago, I...
Years later, I...

young *adjective*
When I was young, I...

Printed in Great Britain
by Amazon